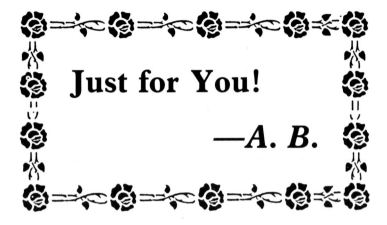

Just for You!

—A. B.

Endpaper photographs by Frank Nothaft
Frontispiece by Dr. E. J. Mulawka

A Beginner's Guide to
Cockatoos

Written by
Annmarie Barrie

Contents

© 1986 by T.F.H. Publications, Inc. Distributed in the UNITED STATES by T.F.H. Publications, Inc., 211 West Sylvania Avenue, Neptune City, NJ 07753; in CANADA by H & L Pet Supplies Inc., 27 Kingston Crescent, Kitchener, Ontario N2B 2T6; Rolf C. Hagen Ltd., 3225 Sartelon Street, Montreal 382 Quebec; in CANADA to the Book Trade by Macmillan of Canada (A Division of Canada Publishing Corporation), 164 Commander Boulevard, Agincourt, Ontario M1S 3C7; in ENGLAND by T.F.H. Publications Limited, 4 Kier Park, Ascot, Berkshire SL5 7DS; in AUSTRALIA AND THE SOUTH PACIFIC by T.F.H. (Australia) Pty. Ltd., Box 149, Brookvale 2100 N.S.W., Australia; in NEW ZEALAND by Ross Haines & Son, Ltd., 18 Monmouth Street, Grey Lynn, Auckland 2 New Zealand; in SINGAPORE AND MALAYSIA by MPH Distributors (S) Pte., Ltd., 601 Sims Drive, #03/07/21, Singapore 1438; in the PHILIPPINES by Bio-Research, 5 Lippay Street, San Lorenzo Village, Makati Rizal; in SOUTH AFRICA by Multipet Pty. Ltd., 30 Turners Avenue, Durban 4001. Published by T.F.H. Publications, Inc. Manufactured in the United States of America by T.F.H. Publications, Inc. © 1986 by T.F.H. Publications, Inc. Ltd.

1.
Introduction

Of the approximately 340 species of parrots, half are found in Australia and the Pacific islands, 140 in Central and South America and the Caribbean, and the remainder in Africa and southern Asia. Currently, seventeen species of cockatoos are recognized, and divided

These two sulphur-crested cockatoos show that the subspecies do vary considerably in size. Photo by Steve Kates.

into thirty-eight subspecies. All are native to Australia and some of the islands of the South Pacific.

All parrots have several common characteristics: hooked bills, a comparatively large skull, a thick tongue adapted for grasping, special feathers called powder downs, and feet with two toes facing forward and two facing backward, enabling the foot to serve as an effective grasping mechanism.

Though members of the family Cacatuidae (cockatoos) vary tremendously in size and appearance, they do exhibit many similar features. All cockatoos have a bald spot on the top of the head, covered by an erectile crest. Except for the Cockatiel, cockatoos have short, bobbed tails, and all cockatoos have strong bills made of hardened keratin. Depending on the species, the beaks are colored either beige or black. All have periphthalmic rings of white, blue, or purple. The powder downs beneath the outer layer of plumage provide insulation to regulate the body temperature. They break down into a thick powder used as a waterproof, protective coating and for cleaning the outer feathers. You can rub your hand on the feathers of a cockatoo and have it coated with powder. The feet of an adult may be white, gray or black.

Cockatoos become sexually mature around eight years of age and will continue to reproduce in to their twenties and thirties. Their life expectancy is thirty to fifty years, and some have survived in captivity for sixty to seventy years. Both male and female cockatoos, unlike most other parrots, actively participate in the incubation and feeding of their young.

Due to their longevity, personality, and cleverness, cockatoos are popular as pets and breeding birds. Not

Goffin's, one of the smaller cockatoos, is now more available to bird keepers than it used to be. Photo by Glen S. Axelrod.

only are they beautiful; cockatoos are intelligent, affectionate, and loyal. Their royal behavior, calmness, and grandeur have made them striking exhibition birds at many shows.

Even though there is a great demand for cockatoos, the Australian government is very strict in refusing to export them for the pet trade, despite the fact the birds enjoy feeding on cultivated fields.

Because of the great demand, low supply, and sky-rocketing prices, smugglers bring birds into the country illegally. Regulations for importing birds, including quarantining them for a specified time, are meant to prevent the diseases that can be carried by the birds. Smugglers ignore the laws; concealment and transport of smuggled birds result in a great amount of stress, resulting in an even greater incidence of disease and death. Infections are then passed on to other birds with which they come into contact.

Many parrots are included on the endangered species list; however, no cockatoos are presently listed. Many of the jungle habitats from which cockatoos originate have been deforested, burned, or in some other way altered or ravaged so the animals can no longer survive there. Because of this, aviculturists must be allowed to keep and breed all kinds of cockatoos to secure their survival for future generations.

2.
Cockatoos as Pets

When deciding on any pet for the home, it is imperative that the advantages of having a pet and its drawbacks as well are taken into consideration before the purchase. An animal, its home, and its owners must all be suitable

The white cockatoos, like this Salmon-crested, have colors in their plumage that are not always conspicuous. Photo by P. Leysen.

and compatible for all the parties involved to be happy, healthy, and thriving.

Being docile, intelligent, long-lived, and spectacular in appearance, cockatoos are popular pets. Most are very adaptable animals, but some require a long period of adjustment in a new home. Of course, young birds are more docile and easier to tame, but do not overlook an older bird that displays a good disposition. With cockatoos, as opposed to some other birds, sex is not an important consideration. Both males and females make equally wonderful pets. If you are selecting birds for breeding purposes, though, then be sure to obtain birds of the right sexes. Fortunately, as breeders, cockatoos are easier to work with than amazons, macaws, and other larger parrots.

Most cockatoos are intelligent and quick to learn, and therefore a great source of entertainment. Some are such nervous creatures that their intelligence is quite difficult to perceive. With plenty of time and patience, your cockatoo is very capable of being tamed and trained. Handled properly, they become rather affectionate and loyal animals, loving to be stroked and spoken to. But when mistreated, cockatoos can become dangerous characters with a severe bite. Unless you have had ample and successful experience with smaller parrots, do not buy a cockatoo. They require a great deal of attention, plenty of room, and often they make a lot of noise.

Cockatoos have impressive vocal abilities, which can be quite disturbing to your neighbors. The birds insist upon welcoming the sunrise, no matter how early in the day it arrives. And being such loyal comrades, they may screech loudly and harshly in your absence while waiting for your return, or they may pull out their feathers in protest.

Cockatoos do not have a reputation for being good talkers, but with proper and consistent coaching, they can master a number of words and sounds. Their abilities are surprisingly extensive, though the quality of the voice is not as cultured as that of some other parrots.

Being clean birds, cockatoos require little maintenance. Their cages do need regular cleaning, and food and water need to be changed daily. They are hardy birds, yet cockatoos are susceptible to drafts and can pick up human infections. Use thought and care when handling any bird, because caring for a sick bird is more difficult than caring for a healthy one.

To stay in optimum condition, all birds need exercise. Your pet should be provided with a large, roomy cage, and allowed ample time for free-flying indoors. A confined bird can become bored, frustrated, or ill. A flying area of ample size, void of heavy and easily overturned objects, should be available. Cockatoos, like other parrots, take great pleasure in chewing and gnawing, especially wood. Always supervise your bird when it is uncaged, and protect chewable items: furniture, important papers, plants (some may even be poisonous to your bird) and anything else that you would prefer not to be destroyed. A cockatoo should never be left alone with an undisciplined child or an inexperienced handler. They are dangerous to one another.

Cockatoos can be left alone for a couple of days with the right provisions, but for an extended trip, arrangements must be made with a reliable friend or relative to visit

Salmon-crested Cockatoos, Cacatua moluccensis, *housed outdoors in a zoological garden. Photo by Dr. Herbert R. Axelrod.*

the bird. The water and food containers need to be freshened, the cage cleaned, and the bird exercised.

Each cockatoo has a definite and individual personality. Most are naturally outgoing and quickly tamed, others are moody and temperamental. Some are shy and withdrawn, others bold and daring. Cockatoos, though, may take some time before they reveal their true personality—a bird timid or overly demonstrative at first may prove to be a wonderfully well-adjusted pet.

3.
Selection

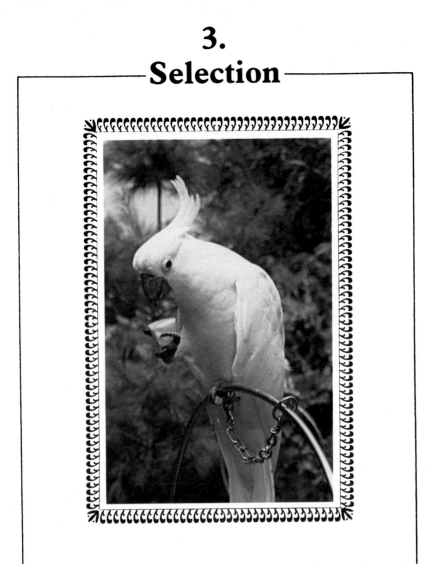

Each species of cockatoo has its own particular characteristics. Familiarize yourself with these traits before your purchase to be certain that you are getting the bird you want. For example, let me describe to you what

Not renowned as talkers, cockatoos are mostly enjoyed for their antic behavior. Photo by Steve Kates.

cockatoos are perhaps best known for; the crest. Some are large and some small, in a variety of colors. Crests can curve backwards or forwards; some are noticeable at rest, while others are inconspicuous until raised. Cockatoos are able to erect their crest at will, whether they be irritated, nervous, excited, or happy. Most of the birds will display their crests during courtship.

Needless to say, don't buy the first bird that you see. Consult a reference book detailing the descriptions of all cockatoos. Bring it with you as a guide as you examine the cockatoos on display.

A variety of stores and breeders sell cockatoos. If you purchase through a breeder, choose one with a long-standing reputation for quality breeding. He knows a lot about his birds and will not sell an inferior specimen that may mar his reputation. Quite possibly his birds have been hand-reared and will be rather tame. These cockatoos are people-oriented; they will not be distracted by other birds and will develop a strong bond with their owner. A tame bird will calmly step on and off your arm, refrain from biting, and not flutter if you touch it.

If you buy your pet from a pet shop, choose a dealer with good inventory and clean, neat cages. He obviously cares well for his birds and can provide you with all the proper supplies. Seek out well-informed employees, because they are the ones you will rely on for sound advice. A reputable dealer can tell you about the background of your bird, and quite likely your selection will have been bred locally.

Observe the cockatoo for as long as possible. It is imperative that the bird you select is healthy. It is easier to

16

Major Mitchell's Cockatoo is remarkable for the splendid coloration of its crest.
Photo by Dr. Gerald R. Allen.

maintain a healthy cockatoo than it is to nurse a sick one. Although many diseases cannot be detected in the early stages, a little knowledge about some of the symptoms displayed can be invaluable.

Make sure the cockatoo looks alert and not puffed up. Note any prolonged periods of lethargy or restlessness. A sleepy, drowsy look can mean the bird is tired, but it can also be an indication of illness. The eyes should be bright and clear, with no evidence of discharge. Frequent closing of the eyes and contracted pupils are signs of injury or infection. There should be no lumps or scratches around the eye ring. The bird should sit erect on its perch, with a sleek, well-groomed appearance. The wings should not be held out from the body, nor should they droop. The plumage should be full, with no bare spots anywhere except the crown. Any more damage than a couple of broken feathers are signs of a feather chewer. Do not accept a bird with sores or wounds. There should be no lumps at the base of the feathers. If the bird's wing feathers have been clipped, check to see that it has been done properly.

Take note of the bird's respiration; it should be slow and even—not rapid, irregular, or labored. The nostrils must be clean and open. No discharge or dirt should be on the feathers around the cere; these feathers should be smooth, dry, and in place. The nostrils should be round and regularly shaped, not extending into the beak or showing any redness or irritation.

The beak should be nicely shaped, with the mandibles coming together nicely. It should not be overgrown or deformed. White or yellow spots on the beak or legs are an indication of fungus or injury.

The Little Corella, Cacatua sanguinea, *is one of the most abundant cockatoos in its native Australia. Photo by A. J. Mobbs.*

The feet should be in good condition, with both feet displaying equal grasping strength. One missing toe is not usually a problem, but if a bird favors a leg, pass that specimen over. If you can feel the cockatoo's feet, check that there is even heat in both. A cool foot can be a problem.

Have the dealer hold the bird so you can feel the breast. It should be firm, full, and plump. The breast bone should not protrude.

Observe the bird's droppings on the cage floor. They should be firm, not loose and watery, and a mixture of dark green and white—not bright green, brown, black, yellow, or orange, all of which indicate a digestive disorder. The feathers around the vent must be clean, not soiled.

Both male and female cockatoos make equally satisfactory pets. If you need to determine the sex for some reason, as in mating, it is generally simple. Except for bare-eyed cockatoos and related species, females exhibit red or reddish-brown eyes, while the eyes of males are very dark or black. It is more difficult to differentiate between a young and an older cockatoo, but most birds under one-and-a-half years of age have light gray eyes. Immature birds are often mistaken for females. A few species of cockatoos do have obvious differences according to sex, but this does not hold true for most.

Be prepared to pay a respectable price for your cockatoo. Aspects such as rarity, whether the bird is domestically raised or imported, tame or wild determine the cost. Birds that already display talking ability fetch a higher price than a non-proven talker.

Some birds are less expensive because they are sold as

imperfect, but healthy. Handicaps, such as a blind eye, drooped wing, or crooked leg, do not prevent a cockatoo from becoming a delightful pet. Certainly you need not pay a premium price for an imperfect bird. It is a good idea to have these birds checked by a veterinarian to ensure that the disability is not worse than it appears.

You may want to have your new pet examined by a veterinarian immediately before bringing it home, even if the bird seems perfect. Arrange with the dealer for a refund or exchange if the bird is found to be unhealthy. Do not hesitate to return your cockatoo to the dealer if it becomes ill in the first few days. The more time that elapses, the less responsibility will be taken by him.

Your cockatoo will probably be placed in a box so that you can bring it home. Have its cage prepared in advance to minimize the time the bird spends in the box.

Do not transport the bird on a cold, windy, or damp day. These factors increase the chances of your cockatoo becoming ill. Keep the bird warm, avoiding any rapid changes in temperature. The journey itself will be trauma enough, so try to eliminate any additional and unnecessary stress.

Try to bring your bird home early in the day so it has time to adjust and recoup from the stress of transport before nightfall. This also allows you time to thoroughly re-examine the bird at home. Do not panic, though, if your new pet stays still for prolonged periods of time. This is a normal reaction for any bird that just needs some time to relax and settle in.

A newly acquired cockatoo may refuse to eat for the first day or two. Do not let this upset you. If more time passes, call the dealer and ascertain if your food offerings are not significantly different from that which was previously provided. Keep in mind that some birds simply prefer to eat privately, when no humans are present.

An untame bird may shiver when it is closely watched. This merely indicates an unfamiliarity with human contact.

If you lack experience handling such large birds, just keep in mind that the bird is probably more afraid of you! Use a firm but gentle approach when taking the cockatoo from the box and placing it in the cage. Never grip the animal by the throat, legs, or tail. Always support the full weight of its body or you could unintentionally inflict some damage. Wearing thin gloves, or wrapping your fingers with adhesive strip or tape really won't give much protection if the bird decides to snap and bite. In fact, this may frighten the bird even more. If you prefer, you can line up the opening of the box close to the cage door and let the bird hop in itself. If the cockatoo does happen to fly free, secure it in a net or with a light towel or cloth.

Continually talk and whistle softly to the bird to calm it. A relaxed cockatoo adapts quickly to its new surroundings, making it easy to tame and train. If you already own birds and are introducing a new one to the group, isolate the new bird for at least thirty days. Sixty would be even better. Signs of illness may take some time to present themselves. Quarantining prevents the spread of diseases and parasites. During this time, note any distress, weakness, and lack of appetite. Start immediately with a high protein, high vitamin diet.

4.
Housing

Cockatoos are fair-sized birds, with large wing spans. They may be used to wide-open spaces, so they need roomy and comfortable quarters. Aviaries outdoors are the largest and most expensive housing, but they are the

Sulphur-crested Cockatoos—pet birds may be allowed time outdoors, provided they are supervised.
Photo by Steve Kates.

most suitable for your bird, and will prove to be convenient for you. Only aviaries provide enough space for a free-flying captive bird.

Cockatoos can fully adjust to the temperature changes of a temperate climate if they are introduced to it in mid-summer. By winter, they will be fully acclimated. If temperatures do drop below 40 degrees, and the aviary is not heated, it is wise to bring a cockatoo indoors.

Aviaries can be constructed of wood, metal piping, glass, fiberglass, or other material. If wood is used, wire should be fastened to the wood as a guard against a cockatoo's avid chewing. Metal may be costlier initially, but in the long run may be cheaper because it won't have to be replaced. Metal is also easier to keep clean. An aviary can be any shape, and the size is determined by the number of birds you plan to keep.

The aviary must be rodent-proof, and the floor should be easy to clean and disinfect. It should be partially shaded so the bird can shield itself from too much strong sunlight. Provide a sheltered area that will protect a bird from the elements.

Ideally, the aviary should have a double door preventing accidental escape of the cockatoo as you exit or enter. The doors should be kept locked, with the latch on the outside to prevent the bird from opening it.

Most pet cockatoos will be housed indoors. Cages do not provide the flight and exercise room of an aviary, but a cockatoo can flourish just as well, given the proper consideration. Of course, the larger the cage, the better. It should be at least large enough for your cockatoo to fully extend its wings. Look at cages suitable for a large macaw or a large monkey. The idea is to avoid having the wing and tail feathers rub on the bars, making them frayed.

Select a metal cage with thick, sturdy wires. Remember that cockatoos love to chew, so a wooden cage would soon be destroyed and too-thin wire can be distorted. Horizontal wires allow the bird to climb up and down the sides of the cage as a pastime. Make sure the wires are not far enough apart for the bird to stick its head through. Your pet may scrape its head and eyes or, worse, become entrapped and thereby strangle. Do not coat the wires with plastic or paint that can be chewed off and cause digestive disorders.

The cage door should be large enough for you to remove the bird as it rests on your hand without touching any part of the opening.

Cages usually come with seed and water containers. Do not position any dishes beneath perches. A properly constructed cage has provisions for securing cups to the side of the cage, which makes the containers easily accessible to the birds, avoids tipping, and lessens the possibility of droppings contaminating the contents. It is likely that such a cage will also have doors for each dish to facilitate their being cleaned and refilled. The cups need to be washed daily with soap and hot water before fresh food is supplied.

Do not crowd your cockatoo with accessory items. If the cage does not come with perches, buy wooden ones or make them from tree branches. A large cockatoo will rest comfortably on a perch two to three inches in diameter, while a small cockatoo will prefer a diameter of one to two inches. Two or three perches, of varying sizes, will exercise the feet and legs. Periodically clean the perches with a brush, fine sandpaper, or a perch scraper to loosen any debris. If you wet them, let the perches dry completely before placing them back in the cage. Wet or damp perches can cause arthritis, rheumatism, and colds. Position perches far enough from the sides of the cage so the wing and tail feathers do not rub against them; also allow for plenty of head room.

A simple toy may be appreciated by your cockatoo. Toys, bells, and mirrors can be clipped in the cage for amusement. Table-tennis balls or a thick tree branch that can be chewed and splintered are great fun. Be creative and change the toys periodically. Cockatoos are such phenomenal chewers that anything made of wood will soon be destroyed. Keep a constant supply of wood available to prevent the bird from chewing on the wrong things. Safest and most enjoyable for your cockatoo are products such as Nylarings and Nylabird Dumbbells and Perch Rings, available at your local pet shop.

You may wish to set up a play ground. Outside of the cage. Be sure it has no sharp edges, no small pieces that can be broken off and swallowed, and that none of the materials are toxic.

A grid in the lower part of the cage will prevent a cockatoo from walking in its own droppings, and it keeps out of reach any food that has fallen and become old and soiled. Be sure the grid openings are too small for a bird to trap its head but large enough that it doesn't catch its feet or toes. Line the cage floor with paper, and cover that with sand, ground corncob, or other material for extra absorbency. Replace this litter every few days or whenever the mess makes you uncomfortable. Some cages come with a removable metal tray to facilitate cleaning. Wash and dry the cage floor weekly, and periodically wipe the cage bars. Scrubbing with a stiff brush will loosen stubborn debris.

For the first couple of days, you may want to place the cage in a quiet room, like a spare bedroom. This is only meant to be temporary, until the bird settles in. When the bird is more calm and relaxed, you can move the cage to a more busy room. Depending on your intuition and personality of the cockatoo, you may prefer to place the bird in its permanent location immediately. A room in which you spend a lot of your time is suggested, like a living room or den. Avoid kitchens, where drastic temperature changes are common. Daytime temperatures should average between 65 and 80 degrees. Nighttime temperatures can be as low as the high 40s.

The cage area should be free of smoke and fumes. It should have good ventilation, yet be away from drafty windows and doors. Birds kept indoors have a thinner coat of down and so are more susceptible to chills. Do not place the cage too near radiators and heaters which are drying and damaging to the plumage.

If the cage is subject to direct sunlight sometime during the day, be sure the exposure is not too excessive, and that there is always a shaded area where the bird may seek repose. An area that has indirect natural light throughout the day is probably the best choice.

Placement of the cage with regard to height should be considered. A cage that is too high denies the bird optimum human contact. Too low a cage may make a cockatoo feel insecure. Overhead movement means danger to your bird; in the wild, danger from predators comes from above. Eye level is preferred, so the bird feels secure yet has a lot of exposure to human activity.

In their natural habitat, cockatoos are used to a twelve-hour day. At night, the room should be quiet and dark so the bird can get sufficient rest. If this is not possible, a drape or cloth placed over the cage will do as well. This cloth also serves to calm the bird should it become noisy or anxious. Simply drape it over the cage until the cockatoo is quiet; then remove it. A well-behaved bird should never be left covered, for it may have only been trying to attract your attention, which is a common occurrence with cockatoos. Of course, you may have an unusual schedule and will prefer not to cover the bird while you are at home. Many birds can adapt themselves to your routine by napping while you are out of the house.

A pair of Red-vented Cockatoos are being given a spray bath. Photo by Dr. E. W. Burr.

The Salmon-crested, or Moluccan, Cockatoo is much in demand as a pet. Photo by Steve Kates.

Because of their playfulness, cockatoos respond well to trick training. Photo by Dr. Herbert R. Axelrod.

If you would like to bring your caged cockatoo outdoors, hang the cage from a tree out of direct sunlight and out of the reach of potential predators. A pet bird outdoors needs constant supervision. Only if the area is known to be free of danger can the cage be set upon the ground. Remember that your caged cockatoo is a helpless victim and cannot flee from any harm that may come along.

All pet birds should be allowed flying opportunities indoors. They need the exercise to keep fit and trim. A suggested alternative to keeping your pet caged all the time is to use a stand. Cockatoos are not as active as other parrots and are rather content to remain on a stand. It can be bought or made easily. If you let your bird remain on the stand for extended periods, water and food dishes, along with some chew toys, can be attached to it. Place a box or some protective sheets under the stand to catch all seeds and droppings. It is best not to restrict the bird to the stand all the time. On a stand, a cockatoo cannot climb as it likes to do in a cage, and a stand lacks the safety of a cage.

5.
Feeding

A balanced diet and plenty of exercise circumvents many diseases and breeding disorders. If a bird does become ill, a disease will have a more deleterious effect on a poorly nourished body. It is important to offer your

The Palm Cockatoo, Probosciger aterrimus, *largest of all the cockatoos, belongs to the group of black cockatoos. Photo by Dr. Herbert R. Axelrod.*

31

cockatoo a varied diet of seeds, greens, and animal protein to insure that it receives all the essential proteins, fats, carbohydrates, vitamins, and minerals necessary for maintaining a healthy body and for reproduction. Cockatoos sometimes eat poorly; they must te taught to eat properly. Commercial seed mixtures contain sunflower seeds, safflower, hard corn, peanuts and red peppers, providing most of the protein, fats, and carbohydrates needed by your bird. A large number of vitamins and minerals are obtained from fruits, vegetables, and greens, which are also a good source of fiber and roughage.

Meat, fish, milk, cheese, peanut butter, and eggs are prime sources of protein, essential for the formation and maintenance of body tissues. Protein aids in the production of keratin, used in the formation of the beak, feathers, and claws.

Fats store energy, are necessary for the proper absorption of some vitamins, and help to heat, insulate, and protect against injury. Too little fat results in dry skin and feathers. Good sources of fat are seeds, fish oils, and eggs.

Seeds, cereal, grains, and fruit contain carbohydrates, and the roughage they provide aids in digestion.

Vitamins

Vitamin A is required for the normal development of bone structure and in building immunity against disease. It also aids in proper growth, good vision, and maintenance of healthy skin and mucous membranes. Foods rich in vitamin A include apples, carrots, corn, meat, fish, eggs, milk, and milk products. Greens like dandelions, celery, spinach, and lettuce, as well as fruits like bananas and tomatoes, are also high in vitamin A.

The vitamins in the B complex are required for growth and hatchability. Vitamin B is crucial in the metabolism of fats and carbohydrates and for the maintenance of the nervous system. The best sources of vitamin B are yeast and wheat germ (already contained in some commercial foods) and whole-wheat bread.

Vitamin C, found especially in citrus fruits, is involved in the production of connective tissue.

Important in the production of keratin, vitamin D is also critical during breeding for the formation of eggshells. Vitamin D is involved in the production of bone and is responsible for regulating the balance of certain minerals. Synthesized by the skin from direct sunlight, eggs and fish oils are also good sources of this vitamin.

Other vitamins, as well as minerals, are just as important to a healthy bird. A lack of any one of them can cause severe problems, which is why a rich and varied diet is necessary. This does not mean you should give your cockatoo table scraps, which can cause digestive disorders.

Fruits with the greatest abundance of vitamins and minerals are apples, bananas, oranges, peaches, and pears. These can be wedged between the wires of the cage. Probably the most valuable vegetables are carrots, celery, corn, kale, dandelions, and spinach. An inexpensive way to provide fresh foods the year round is to work out an arrangement with your local dealer for fresh produce scraps. Wash them all thoroughly, and do not offer them to your pet if they are not fresh enough for you to eat yourself. Greens can be secured to the cage wires with a clothespin.

Fresh tree branches satisfy a cockatoo's gnawing instinct, also providing good nutrition. Local weeds and grasses, if not treated with insecticides or fouled by other animals, can be collected and offered to your pet. It is a good idea not to leave any of these greens, fruits, or vegetables overnight because they may spoil by morning. Wilted and rotten foods are dangerous to your cockatoo.

New foods

Cockatoos may not readily accept new foods. Offer them anyway, even if it seems your bird does not eat them. Introduce new foods gradually, and one at a time. Too much change could upset its digestion. Allow your bird to pick and choose, and soon you will be able to identify its tastes. A suggested daily feeding program includes seeds, one green and one yellow vegetable, and two fruits. Pumpkin seeds, watermelon seeds, pistachio nuts, and the like can be used as treats. Occasionally, a few drops of wheat-germ oil or cod-liver oil can be added to the seed.

Periodically check the freshness of the seed. Sample a few seeds by tasting them; they should be sweet and nutty, not bitter. Another test is to sprout the seed. Soak it for twenty-four hours in water, then place it on a damp paper towel. In a day or two, seeding grasses should appear, which you may feed to your bird. If the seed does not sprout, then it is not suitable food dry either. Seed soaked for twenty-four hours is not only rendered more digestible (an advantage to chicks in the nest) but is a useful variation to the diet. Soaking has

It's desirable that a stand has provision for feeding just as a cage does. Photo by P. Leysen.

altered the food value because the seed has undergone the chemical changes which naturally accompany germination. The vitamin and protein levels have been increased. Prepare only small amounts at a time because soaked seed spoils quickly.

No more than a three-to-four week supply of any seed should be kept on hand. With time, seeds dry out and lose nutritional value. Moisture and humidity foster molds, so seal the food in moisture-proof containers in the refrigerator, or some other cool, dry place, to prevent spoilage.

After your cockatoo has adapted to its new home and developed a routine, monitor its food intake over a week. Take note of how much and what kinds of food it eats. In the future, you will be able to recognize any change, which may indicate an illness. While molting, or during cold weather, a cockatoo may need to eat more than usual.

A cockatoo gets a lot of water and moisture from fresh, juicy greens, but drinking water should always be present. You may wish to fortify it with a liquid vitamin supplement once a week or so.

If you follow this regimen, there will be no need for special foods, tonics, or conditioners. A properly cared for bird is likely to remain alive and healthy for many years.

Grit and cuttlebone

Both grit and cuttlebone are sources of essential minerals and trace elements. Grit is stored in the gizzard to assist in the digestion of food. Most cockatoos do not eat the gravel mixtures marketed for smaller birds, but prefer a coarser mixture. This grit, or bird sand, should contain some other organic materials, such as crushed oyster shells. Crushed hard-boiled eggshells work well, too. If they are not already in the mixture, they can be bought separately and added to the grit. These organic compounds are especially important during breeding. Offer the grit in a separate dish from the regular food, and replace it weekly, or more often if it becomes soiled.

Cuttlebone is the internal shell of the cuttlefish, a marine animal closely related to squids. It provides calcium for a firm beak, strong eggshells when breeding, a healthy skeletal structure in the chicks, and prevents egg binding. Gnawing on a cuttlebone, or a similar aviary-sized mineral block, helps to keep the beak from becoming overgrown while a cockatoo satisfies its inclination to chew. Cuttlebone usually comes with a clip, but if it has none, simply punch holes in it. Attach it with wire to the side of the cage near a perch.

Bathing

In the wild, cockatoos are often bathed by rain showers. Most of these birds will enjoy being bathed or sprayed with water from a spray bottle. Bathing not only keeps a bird clean, but it makes the feathers shine and makes its colors more brilliant.

A large dish or bowl can be placed in the cage or out, so the cockatoo can bathe itself. The bird, though, will likely not get a thorough bath, and the result is quite messy. The cage will need to be dried and the litter changed if the bath is given inside. An alternative is to use a spray bottle of room-temperature water. Be sure the sprayer has not been used for anything other than clean water.

Some birds will use a sink for a makeshift bathtub. Here you can squirt them with the sprayer. A cockatoo will extend its wings and spread its tail, trying to catch as much of the water as possible. Many a bird will fly directly to the sink when it hears the sound of running water!

You may even enjoy letting your pet share your shower. Be sure the spray is gentle and not too hot. Be careful of sudden drops in temperature and humidity when the cockatoo leaves the shower for other rooms in the house. Do not use any soap unless the bird has somehow become greased or stained, and then use the mildest "puppy soap" available. Sprinkle a little powder on the feathers and rub with a soft cloth or sponge. Rinse the bird well, removing all the soap. Any residue will dry.

It is best to bathe a cockatoo early in the day to allow sufficient time for it to dry before the cooler nighttime temperatures set in. Keep your pet free from drafts, and do not take the bird outside for at least six hours if the outside temperature is cooler than indoors.

After bathing, a cockatoo will groom and preen itself, readjusting its feathers. Now it will rub its head and face over the powder downs, and spread the powder all over the body.

6.
Training

Clipping a cockatoo's wing feathers will make taming that much easier. Unless the bird is already used to human handling, taming an unclipped bird will be considerably more tiring for you and the bird. Done corectly,

Tame cockatoos, like this Sulphur-crested, will usually allow their feathers to be touched. Photo by Dr. Herbert R. Axelrod.

wing clipping is not painful to the bird, nor is it permanent. In a few months, the flight feathers will be fully regrown, and you may want to reclip them. Feather clipping is not cruel, nor does it disable the bird. It merely limits its flying ability, causing it to lose its balance and land after traveling only a few feet. When the bird is let out of the cage, there is no possibility of its escaping.

Never attempt to clip a cockatoo without viewing the procedure as performed by an experienced pet handler or veterinarian. Many cockatoos can fly with an under-clipped or improperly clipped wing; but the clipping must not be so extensive that the bird is subject to injury from falls. Having a cockatoo clipped at the pet shop or in a vet's office also prevents the bird from associating a bad experience with its new home.

Two people are required for the procedure. One holds the bird while the other clips. The holder must be calm enough to hold the cockatoo securely and properly. The body of the bird should be fully supported on your lap or a table. Place your thumb under the lower mandible and your second and third fingers around the head to keep the neck straight without pushing or pulling the head. If you grab the bird incorrectly you may break its neck or have your finger bitten. Turn the bird on its back, and with your other hand hold the feet and torso. Monitor the bird's respiration and pupils for any signs of distress or shock.

Clipping only one wing results in the cockatoo losing control over its flight direction. This facilitates taming because a bird is more easily discouraged from fleeing when it cannot fly where it intends.

Under good light, extend each wing from the bend to determine which one will be cut. Leave the better feathered wing alone. Next check for blood feathers. These are new feathers, still growing in, and nourished by a blood vessel running through the center. This vessel is sealed off in a fully grown feather. Identify blood feathers before clipping so they will not be cut and therefore bleed. If you do cut one, treat it with hydrogen peroxide and apply styptic powder.

Push back the covert feathers to expose the quill of each feather. Using barber scissors or a small pair of wire cutters, trim the feathers straight across the quill, leaving at least two inches of feather protruding from the wing. Leaving the outermost two or three primary feathers unclipped preserves the long, graceful appearance of the wings when they are in a resting position.

After your pet is tamed, you may or may not want to keep it clipped. Periodically check for regrowth, and once you know the bird's flying habits, you can alter the number of clipped feathers.

Taming

A cockatoo's intellectual capacity includes understanding simple commands, and speaking words and phrases. With gentle, consistent training from a serious trainer, most cockatoos will respond favorably in a short period of time. They will become tame and are capable of learning a variety of tricks. Hand-reared chicks may be easier to tame and train because they are accustomed to human contact, but this does not mean that a wild bird with proper training will be any less affectionate or gentle over time.

The first step in taming any bird is to gain its trust. Approach the cage slowly but deliberately, speaking softly to keep the bird calm. Initially, do not attempt to touch the bird, simply allow it to adjust to your approach. When you can come close to the bird without creating a great deal of excitement, open the cage door and attempt to stroke the bird. Do not place your hand near the head or beak (cockatoos do bite when nervous or angry) but start with the bird's feet, tail, or wing feathers. Work your way up to scratching the head. Stick and hand-taming can now begin, either in or out of the cage.

Have a family member with plenty of time and motivation do the initial taming. One trainer is less confusing for the bird. Every day, several short lessons, 20 to 30 minutes at most, need to be given. Short lessons prevent the bird from becoming overtired and losing interest. Lessons every day maintains continuity. If too much time passes between lessons, training will proceed more slowly, and some steps may have to be relearned. The more a bird is used to human handling, the easier it is to train further. Use your own judgement to set the pace, because each cockatoo has its own temperament.

The best taming area is a small room, like a bathroom or closet. Cover all mirrors, and close all windows and doors to prevent escape. Preferably, the room will be devoid of any high spots to perch and will have a minimum of furniture that the bird can hide under or behind. This makes retrieval easier. Be sure there are no objects that can be tipped over or banged into. If the room does not have a rug, cover the floor with some towels or padding to soften any falls and to provide traction. Only the trainer should be in the room with the cockatoo; the less extraneous activity there is, the less distraction for the bird.

A Salmon-crested Cockatoo in the course of stick training. Photo by Dr. Herbert R. Axelrod.

The trainer should wear clothing that is not easily snagged by a cockatoo's beaks or claws. Do not entice the bird with any hanging clothing, jewelry, or hair that can be grabbed or bitten.

Have ready a low bird stand stable enough to support a cockatoo without tipping over. Two dowels or training sticks, about an inch and a half in diameter, are also needed.

Work close to the floor to prevent long falls. Drill the bird to step on and off the training stick. If the bird refuses to step up or turns away, be persistent, but don't badger it. Touch the bird gently with the stick, pushing it into the bird's belly so the bird loses balance and is forced to step up to remain steady. Repeatedly have the cockatoo step from the floor to the stick and back again.

This Sulphur-crested Cockatoo can certainly be described as hand-tame! Photo by Steve Kates.

Slowly raise the stick from the floor and then offer the other dowel as a perch. Reward the bird with praise, petting, and food. A treat of its favorite seed works well. Ignore any unwanted behavior, and soon the bird will catch on. If you work slowly and patiently, allowing the bird plenty of time to become accustomed to your presence, it is likely you will never be bitten. If your cockatoo does attempt to bite, do not strike it. Remove your hand and loudly say "NO!" Do not excite or frighten the bird any further.

When the bird is comfortable with stick taming, introduce it to the stand. Drill the cockatoo in the same manner, from the stick to the stand and back again. A simple rolling motion of the stick forces the bird to step forward to regain a foothold. If your cockatoo continually jumps from the stand, keep returning it to the stand until it learns to stay.

When your cockatoo is comfortable with passing from the stand to the stick, substitute your arm for the dowel. If the bird is timid, press your arm into its belly to force it to step, using your other hand to distract it from biting. Soon you will be able to walk around the taming area with the bird perched on your arm. The cockatoo may begin to walk up your arm to your shoulder—a parrot always tries to get to the highest possible position. Also remember that there is no such thing as a housebroken bird!

Train the cockatoo for longer sessions each day. You'll notice how quickly it reacts to attention. Introduce other family members by allowing them to feed and play with the bird. After a lesson, offer the cockatoo plenty of food and water. It will probably be tired and very thirsty. Feeding a cockatoo only in its cage or on its stand will train it to return there when hungry. If you want the bird to return to its cage on command, filling a dish with fresh food is very enticing.

Allowing a cockatoo to come out of the cage for exercise and attention will ensure better health and make it friendlier toward people. Always supervise the bird during its free time to prevent it from chewing furniture, plants, and wallpaper. Provide lots of chew toys for distraction.

The least you should expect from a tame bird is to have it rest comfortably on your hand without biting or fleeing. With the bird feeling safe and secure in your hands, it will be easier to examine and treat it should it become ill.

Young birds are usually easier to tame, but you may

have purchased an older bird. These cockatoos may be more frightened and require more time and patience, but they can still make wonderful pets. Or, you may have bought a bird from someone who can no longer keep it. Even if these birds are tame, they may be slow to accept a new owner; you may not have to go through the formalities of basic taming, but lots of hours of consistent and patient handling may be required.

The most effective way to change a bird's behavior is to put in lots of time. Occasionally, a bird comes along that cannot be handled, but don't cheat on the taming time and blame the bird for your lack of persistence. Give the bird to someone else, but don't pass the bird off to a person without detailing the behavior problems. Try to find the best possible home for the cockatoo; someone else may be able to relate to it better. Talk to zoos and breeders who are more concerned with how a bird relates to other birds than how it relates to people.

Simple tricks

Advanced training requires a reward system of positive reinforcement. Acknowledge all desired behavior with a reward of acknowledgement, affection, or food. Disregard any unwanted behavior. A cockatoo can push and pull objects with its beak, or be taught tricks like laying its head down in your hand. A bird will gently have to be shown what to do, and then rewarded. Doing this repeatedly helps the bird to associate the response with its performance.

Even natural behavior, like spreading its wings, can be performed on command. Simply pick up the bird's wing and say, "Lift your wing." Scratch the bird or offer a food reward, and soon when you say the phrase, the

The underside of the wing of the Salmon-crested Cockatoo is yellow, with a salmon tinge. Photo by Dr. Herbert R. Axelrod.

bird will lift its wing in anticipation of a reward. When the bird has mastered one trick, introduce another, capitalizing on its natural antics, like waving the wing, raising the foot, bobbing the head, and putting items into a container. Do not confuse the bird with too many things at once.

Think of advanced training as an extension of the initial taming. Use the same room and the same trainer. Short sessions, daily lessons, and positive reinforcements of praise and food work best.

Talking

Cockatoos are not renowned for their speaking talents, but no two birds, even of the same species, have the same talking ability. Since cockatoos have such diverse individual personalities, they can only be assessed on an individual basis. Given the right training, a cockatoo can become an excellent talker, mastering many different sounds and phrases. Of course, for many enthusiasts, having a tame, affectionate, and intelligent bird is more important than its ability to talk.

Talking is not guaranteed, and the length of time it will take for your bird to speak is unpredictable. Repetition is the key, but the monotony of teaching causes many people to give up. Again, think of talking as another advanced training trick; develop a uniform schedule of daily training to facilitate learning. Only a tame, rested, and relaxed bird will respond, and it will probably better imitate someone to whom it is attached. Many birds respond more readily to the high-pitched voices of women and children.

Choose a simple word or short phrase, saying it clearly and slowly. A bird has a tendency to repeat a word more rapidly than it is taught. Do not interject extraneous dialogue that may confuse the bird. Keep repeating it every day until the cockatoo responds. At first it may not be clear, so have the bird say it continually until easily understood. Reward appropriate sounds with a treat. When the bird is fluent, introduce a new phrase.

You may want to buy or make a training tape to play when you are not around. However, a cockatoo may learn only to talk when it is alone, never when you are present.

7.
Breeding

Cockatoos must be about five to six years of age for breeding purposes. Be sure to have a male and a female that like one another, or breeding will not occur. Keep

Sulphur-crested Cockatoo, Cacatua galerita. *Photo by Stefan Norberg and Anders Hansson.*

in mind that the entire cycle, from fertilization to weaning of the chicks is about three months. During this time, a great amount of your time will be spent caring for the breeding pair and their chicks. (In many instances, the babies will have to be hand-fed, or one of the babies may be allowed to die by the parents.) Before actually breeding any birds, decide beforehand what will be done with the chicks. If you do not plan to care for the offspring, be sure that friends, relatives, or breeders and dealers are interested in the fruits of your efforts.

At this time it is particularly important to provide a proper diet. Poor nutrition can result in egg binding, illness in the breeding pair, and infertile eggs. In some situations, the parents may refuse or be unable to take care of the young. In addition to the regular diet, more high protein foods are needed; cheeses, milk-soaked bread with honey, buttermilk, cottage cheese, and mashed hardboiled eggs. If you prefer, special nesting foods are available on the market. Some birds will accept it, others not. To induce them to eat it, introduce it mixed in with their regular seed. Once they are accustomed to it, offer it in a separate dish. The food is very rich and fattening but essential. If cockatoos receive only seed at this time, the young may be small and weak, susceptible to disease, and have a shortened life span.

An enclosure conducive to breeding must be available. It must be large enough for the cockatoos to spread their wings and get plenty of exercise. There is little chance of breeding occurring without the proper nest. Preferably two nest boxes should be provided, allowing the birds to choose the one they feel most comfortable with. One should be a large garbage can with the cover sealed on. Large cockatoos get a 20-gallon can with a 7 inch diameter entrance hole, and smaller cockatoos get a 12-gallon can with a 5-inch hole. These entrance holes are large enough for the birds to get through with ease, yet small enough to afford privacy. The hole is placed three inches from the top of the can so the chicks cannot climb out at too early of an age, and the bottoms are bent into a concave shape to prevent the eggs from rolling. The interior is lined with wire netting as an aid in climbing in and out easily. Without it, the birds could still exit and enter, but they would be more clumsy and might be more likely to damage the eggs.

The second type of nest box is a wooden box covered both inside and out with wire (remember, cockatoos are avid chewers). A thick, hollow log is equally suitable.

All nest boxes should contain some soft material about three to six inches deep. Two suggestions are shavings and black greenhouse dirt, or a mixture of shredded sugar cane, peat moss, and pine shavings. The nest boxes are hung as high on the wall as possible and secured so they do not rock, yet in a way that they are easily removed. Provide plenty of chew sticks, like Nylabird pacifiers, to keep the birds from destroying the nest from gnawing.

About the middle of February, cockatoos start their mating ritual. The male struts along the perch, spreading his wings, raising his crest, and fanning his tail. He bobs his head up and sways his body from side to side. He utters a series of chattering sounds not typically heard at any other time. The female crouches low and constantly flutters her wings. After this, the pair mutually preen one another and touch beaks. This courting behavior may take place several times before copulation occurs. During the actual mating, the male grabs the hen by the back of the neck with his beak, then slowly steps onto her back. (It is for this reason a lame bird is usually no good for mating.) They can be observed doing this a number of times throughout the day until egg laying begins.

The female prepares the nest box, and during this time you may notice that she casts out some of the bedding material. It will be about forty-eight hours after fertilization that one or two white eggs are laid per clutch. The second egg is laid two days after the first.

It takes from twenty-two to thirty days for them to hatch (depending on the species), the first egg hatching two days before the second. Both the cock and the hen share the task of incubating the eggs; the male generally sits during the day, and the female relieves him for the

Because cockatoos gnaw, metal cans are frequently offered as nesting facilities. Photo by John Daniel.

night. Always provide bath water for the pair, especially during the last week of incubation. As the birds return to sit on the eggs after bathing, their dampened feathers moisten the egg membranes, which eases the hatching of the chicks.

Let the breeding pair alone as much as possible. Do not bother them except for feeding and cleaning the cage. Too much disturbance at this time may upset the birds and cause problems.

If mating has not occurred in three or four weeks, illness may be suspected. Or a change like a different type of nest box or bedding material can be tried. If all else fails, a new mate is the next choice. If mating took place but no eggs followed, a new hen is probably required. If eggs are laid but they are infertile, then a new male may be needed. Many birds will not accept a new mate during one season, though the following season a change in mates will be less of a problem.

Prior to laying, the female has a lump on the underside of the tail near the vent. She may look ruffled and bloated, with labored breathing. If there are two eggs, they will hatch in the same order in which they were laid. Therefore, the chicks will be at different stages of development.

A baby chick is covered with fluffy yellow down except on the crown of the head. The skin has a bluish tone and sheen, indicating good health and blood circulation.

In many species of cockatoo, unless you remove the chicks and hand-feed them, one of the babies may be allowed to die by the parents. If the chicks are neglected, give them a few drops of water for the first few hours, as they are living on the nutrients of the egg yolk. Restlessness and loud peeping indicate that the chick is hungry. A feeding schedule of every two hours for the next fourteen days is now begun.

The chicks can be fed commercial nestling foods, or you may prepare a mixture yourself consisting of a combination of baby cereals, strained baby-food fruits and vegetables, brewer's yeast, a vitamin-mineral supplement, and honey. Keep the mixture warm in an electric heat-and-serve baby-food dish, feeding it to the chicks with an eyedropper or a small spoon. Gently hold up the chick's head to keep it from bobbing, and fill its crop to within 1/4 inch below the esophagus. Just before the crop is empty is the best time for the next feeding. Wipe the chicks clean with a damp cloth or a cotton swab. Any food that dries on the beak or feathers can be irritating and cause sores. As the beak is quite soft, it should be treated carefully. Too much force could cause a deformity.

If the chicks are totally abandoned by the parents (the parents refuse to brood them), place them in an incubator to keep them warm until their feathers begin to grow and provide insulation. A temperature of 95 degrees is recommended for the first week or so.

Around ten days old, the eyes begin to open, and by the eighteenth day the chicks can see well. Pin feathers emerge by the twelfth day, and at twenty six days the quills begin to open. The beak is becoming harder, and you may introduce soaked seed. As the beak continues hardening, regular seed can be offered.

Handle the chicks often during this time so they become accustomed to human contact. "Pretaming" can begin even while they are still with their parents.

8.
Diseases

Under the right conditions, cockatoos are hardy birds and will thrive in captivity. A clean cage and a proper diet are the most important aspects of preventive maintenance, making illness unlikely. Of course, accidents

The Galah, or Rose-breasted, Cockatoo is a common sight in certain parts of Australia. Photo by P. Leysen.

Tame cockatoos can easily be examined occasionally for any signs of illness. Photo by Wayne Wallace.

and illness can happen, but do not panic. For simple matters, refer to this book and others, your local pet-shop salesperson, or a vet. Do not delay calling in a vet for more serious problems. Allowed to continue un-checked, a simple illness can develop into something more serious, and even fatal.

There are many obvious signs of poor health. Note any changes in your pet's disposition: drowsiness, lethargy, and loss of appetite (weight loss can be rapid and fatal). If a bird droops its wings, it may have a fever or be weak. Fluffed up feathers, an attempt to preserve body heat, means a cockatoo is having difficulty maintaining its body temperature. Changes in the color or consistency of the droppings, or a pasty vent area, all denote sickness. Loss of balance or unsteadiness, and any discharge from the eyes, nostrils, or mouth indicate disease or injury.

Isolate sick birds, away from all others, in a hospital cage. You can buy, rent, or make one yourself. Simply cover all but the front of the regular cage, or a smaller one, with plastic or cloth to prevent drafts, chills, and to block any outside stimulation that may excite your bird. Suspend a light bulb nearby, or place a heating pad under the cage for additional warmth. Keep the temperature between 85 and 90 degrees.

Remove all perches and place the food and water containers on the floor to limit the cockatoo's movement. Since your pet may become even more fussy about what it eats, provide some of its favorites. A balanced diet is still preferred, but keeping the bird eating is even more important.

Keep the bird warm and quiet if it is necessary to transport it to a vet. Avoid sudden temperature changes.

An aquarium atop a heating pad may serve well as a brooder for young birds or as a hospital cage for an ill pet. Photo by Frank Nothaft.

Broken legs and wings

The best idea is to call a vet, because the injury is often more serious than it appears. Broken legs and wings require proper splinting and bandaging for healing. If done incorrectly, a bird may be permanently crippled and unable to breed.

Convulsions

If not due to injury, a convulsion is usually associated with a vitamin B deficiency. Administer liquid multivitamins.

Colds

Symptoms of a cold include lethargy, fluffed feathers, and possible sneezing, coughing, or wheezing. The bird may have a nasal discharge and sore-looking eyes. Limit the greens and juicy fruits, and if the condition persists, call a vet. Not properly treated, a cold can develop into more serious and complicated respiratory infections.

Cuts and open wounds

The bleeding will stop shortly if the damage is not severe. Wash the area with hydrogen peroxide and apply styptic powder. A more critical injury requires a vet.

Overgrown beaks

The upper mandible may grow too long and become distorted, making it difficult for the bird to eat. Great care must be taken in trimming the beak, so it is best to visit a vet. Having lots of chewing opportunities, like Nylabone pacifiers, helps to keep the beak in good condition.

Overgrown claws

Overgrown claws are easily treated at home by cutting very carefully, under a good light, with toenail clippers or dog-claw clippers. If you clip too much, a blood vessel will be damaged and bleeding will occur. Treat it with styptic powder, flour, or cornstarch. After clipping, smooth rough edges with a nail file. Wooden perches help to keep claws trim.

Egg binding

Egg binding mostly results from a lack of calcium in a hen's diet. A hen may come out of the nest box and sit in a corner of the cage all puffed up. Her wings droop and her eyes are closed. Breathing may be labored. Apply a few drops of mineral oil to her vent. For further instructions, consult a vet.

Lice, fleas, and ticks

These external parasites feed on the skin, feathers, and blood of your bird. Their presence is annoying to a cockatoo, causing restlessness, preening, scratching, and biting at the feathers. Disinfect the cage and perches immediately with commercial preparations available in pet shops. Scrub all items with a stiff brush. The vet will prescribe a suitable treatment for the bird.

Heat stroke

Typically caused by a careless owner who left the pet exposed to direct sunlight. If not detected soon enough, chances of recovery are slim. Spray the bird with cool water or rub with a moist cloth or sponge until the bird responds.

Conjunctivitis

The most common eye ailment, conjunctivitis occurs as a watery discharge from the eye, causing a bird to close its eyes often and to blink a lot. The eyelids may become so swollen that temporary blindness results. Apply an antibiotic ointment approved by your vet.

Constipation

This condition is typically the result of a diet lacking fresh, leafy vegetables. Your cockatoo will have difficulty passing droppings, which may be small and hard. Correct the diet, offering greens daily. In more serious cases, your vet may recommend a laxative.

Diarrhea

Your pet sits with fluffed feathers, and loose, watery droppings leave the vent soiled. Diarrhea may result from an improper diet or the consumption of unclean food or water, but more often it is associated with another illness. Check for other diseases and adjust the diet.

Internal parasites

Diarrhea, depression, weight loss, thirst, tremors, convulsions, anemia and other disorders are signs of internal parasites. Microscopic examination of the feces will permit your vet to diagnose the specific parasite and recommend the proper medicine. Because the parasites are passed in the feces, be sure your pet does not eat or drink any contaminated food or water that may reintroduce the parasite into its system.

Going light

Usually a sign of another illness, at times the true cause of this marked weight loss cannot be determined. Offer more fattening foods like oats, sunflower seeds, milk-soaked wheat bread, and corn kernels. Your vet may suggest an appetite stimulant.

Tumors and cysts

Have all lumps under the skin examined by a vet. Some are cancerous and result in death.

Arthritis and rheumatism

Stiffness and cramps are often the result of wet and dirty perches or perches that are too small in diameter to provide a proper grip. After washing the perches, be sure they are completely dry before placing them back into the cage. Perches of various diameters exercise the legs and feet.

Shock, concussion

Usually the result of an injury, like flying into a mirror or window. The bird stops moving and emits crying sounds, or it may be silent. Move the bird to a warm, protected spot and minimize disturbances. Check for any other injuries that may require immediate attention. Leave the bird to rest, placing food and water within its reach. It may take a while for the bird to respond.